W9-CSP-951

BE A FORCE ON THE FIELD
SKILLS, DRILLS, AND PLAYS

RACHEL STUCKEY

CRABTREE
Publishing Company

FOOTBALL SOURCE

Author: Rachel Stuckey

Editors: Marcia Abramson, Petrice Custance

Photo research: Melissa McClellan

Design: T.J. Choleva

Cover design: Samara Parent

Proofreader: Janine Deschenes

Editorial director: Kathy Middleton

Prepress technician: Samara Parent

Print coordinator: Margaret Amy Salter

Consultant: R Ian Smith. President. Ontario Football Alliance

Production coordinated by BlueApple*Works* Inc.

Photographs

Cover: istockphoto.com: © Andrew Rich

Interior: © Andy Cruz: p 11, 13 top, 14, 15 top, 16 left, 17 top, 19 left; Bigstock: © actionsports (p 15 left); jaboardm (p 18 right, 22, 29 top right, 30); iStock: © GlobalStock (p 10); © Pamela Moore (p 18 left); © gpflman (p 25 bottom); Shutterstock.com: © dean bertoncelj (title page); © Glen Jones (title page middle); © wavebreakmedia (TOC); pbombaert (page numbers); © Steve Broer (TOC background); © Herbert Kratky (p 4); Mai Techaphan (p 5 right); © Aspen Photo (p 6–7 top, 7 bottom, 9 top right, 13 bottom right, 17 bottom, 19 top, 20 top left, 21 left, 21 top right, 23 top, 25 top, 28 bottom left, 28 top right, 29 left); © Dennis Ku (p 6 bottom, 12–13 top); © Susan Leggett (p 7 right, 12 right); © Mark Herreid (p 8); © Sean Locke Photography (p 9 middle right); © Mike Flippo (p 9 bottom); © Action Sports Photography (p 12 top left); © Richard Paul Kane (p 20, 28–29 top); © Noel Moore (p 20–21 top); © Fingerhut (p 20–21 bottom); © Debby Wong (p 21 bottom right, 26–27); © Alexey Stiop (p 28–29 bottom); Keystone Press: © Jim Damaske (p 16 right); © Chris Szagola (p 23 bottom); © Fort Worth Star-Telegram (p 24); © Daniel Gluskoter (p 29 bottom right); Public Domain: United States Marine Corps. Cpl. Travis Gershaneck (p 5 left)

Library and Archives Canada Cataloguing in Publication

Stuckey, Rachel, author
    Be a force on the field : skills, drills, and plays / Rachel Stuckey.

(Football source)
Includes index.
Issued in print and electronic formats.
ISBN 978-0-7787-2291-5 (bound).--ISBN 978-0-7787-2299-1
(paperback).--ISBN 978-1-4271-1728-1 (html)

    1. Football--Training--Juvenile literature. I. Title.

GV953.5.S88 2016   j796.332   C2015-907466-5
                                            C2015-907467-3

Library of Congress Cataloging-in-Publication Data

CIP available at the Library of Congress

Crabtree Publishing Company

Printed in Canada/012016/BF20151123

www.crabtreebooks.com   1-800-387-7650

Published in Canada
Crabtree Publishing
616 Welland Ave.
St. Catharines, ON
L2M 5V6

Published in the United States
Crabtree Publishing
PMB 59051
350 Fifth Avenue, 59th Floor
New York, New York 10118

Published in the United Kingdom
Crabtree Publishing
Maritime House
Basin Road North, Hove
BN41 1WR

Published in Australia
Crabtree Publishing
3 Charles Street
Coburg North
VIC 3058

CONTENTS

WIN THE DAY!

FOOTBALL AROUND THE WORLD

Football is a very popular sport in North America. Fans can watch football being played nearly all year long in the National Football League (NFL), the Canadian Football League (CFL), and college football leagues in both the United States and Canada. High school football games are also popular, especially in small towns throughout the United States.

International Game

It may not be as popular outside of North America, but football is watched and played all over the world. The International Federation of American Football governs national football associations in over 70 different countries. Many countries, such as Germany and Australia, have national teams and compete in international championships. There are also some professional leagues in Europe and other regions.

Since 1986, the top teams in Europe have met in the Eurobowl championship game.

Flag Football

Football is a **contact sport** and is usually played wearing padding and helmets. Another version of the game is called flag football. The only equipment needed is a belt with two flags attached. Opposing players end the play by grabbing or tearing off an opponent's flag. Flag football is usually a recreational sport, and is often played by both men and women. The International Women's Flag Football Association hosts tournaments around the world.

Boy and girls ages 3-14 play flag football in many different programs such as i9 Sports, NFL Flag, and U.S. Flag and Touch Football League.

Millions of people play rugby, especially in England. Many colleges have men's and women's teams.

What's in a Name?

Around the world, the name football causes some confusion. Outside of North America, football refers to the game of soccer. People refer to North American football as American football or **gridiron** football. Canadian football, which has different rules, is as old as American football and was developed at the same time. Football has the same origins as modern soccer and rugby, which is a ball sport popular in England since the 1800s. The earliest version of football was first played in universities in both Canada and the United States in the late 1800s.

HOW TO PLAY

Football is played by two teams of 11 players (12 players in Canada). The ball is oval-shaped and pointed on either end. The team with the ball tries to move it down the field by passing it or running with it. They must move the ball at least 10 yards in four attempts called **downs** (three downs in Canada). Each down begins at a **line of scrimmage**—the place where both teams line up across from each other, and the team with the ball **snaps** it into play. The other team defends by physically stopping their opponents through blocking, tackling, and intercepting passes. If the team earns 10 yards, they get to start again at **first down**. Teams score points by moving the ball into the **end zone**, which is the end of the field opposite their own goal, or by kicking it through the opposing team's goal posts.

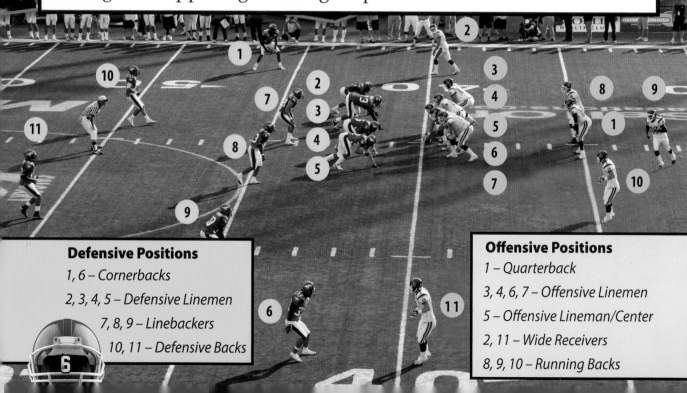

Defensive Positions

1, 6 – Cornerbacks

2, 3, 4, 5 – Defensive Linemen

7, 8, 9 – Linebackers

10, 11 – Defensive Backs

Offensive Positions

1 – Quarterback

3, 4, 6, 7 – Offensive Linemen

5 – Offensive Lineman/Center

2, 11 – Wide Receivers

8, 9, 10 – Running Backs

Football Field

An American football field is 100 yards (91 m) long, plus the two end zones, and is 53⅓ yards (49 m) wide. A football field has white lines every five yards (4.6 m), which makes the field look like a gridiron. **Hashmarks**, or short lines, along the sidelines and down the middle of the field, mark every yard. There are **goal posts** in each end zone.

Winning Points

When a player catches the ball or runs the ball into their opponent's end zone, it is called a touchdown. A touchdown earns six points. Teams can also score three points by kicking

Football players wear special padding on their shoulders, chest, and back. All players wear a helmet with a face mask. Players must also wear shoes with cleats, or spikes.

a **field goal** through the goal posts. After scoring a touchdown, a team gets a chance to score more points. If they run or pass the ball from the scrimmage into the end zone, they earn two more points. If they kick it through the goal posts, they earn one more point.

American vs. Canadian Football Rules

Besides the difference in number of players and downs, the CFL and NFL have some other big differences. For example, in American football the goal posts are at the back of the end zones. In Canadian football, the goal posts are at the front of the end zones. A Canadian football field is also larger—110 yards long by 65 yards wide (101 x 59 m). To score extra points in Canadian football, teams get a point if they kick the ball into the end zone and the opponents cannot kick it out again. This is called a **single** or **rouge**.

Only 11 players per team are allowed on the field at once. Most teams are made up of three different groups: the offense, the defense, and **special teams**.

Specialized Teams

The offense tries to score when their team has possession of the ball. The defense plays against the other team's offense and tries to stop them from scoring. Special teams are on the field whenever there is a kick. They receive the **kickoff** from the other team and are also responsible for kicking field goals and extra points. Special teams will also punt, or kick, the ball down the field on the fourth down (or third down in Canada) if they haven't achieved 10 yards yet.

Football games are divided into quarters and halves. Each team must be ready to take the field quickly because the clock is always running. The time clock only stops in football when there is an **incomplete pass**, a player steps out of bounds, the refs call a penalty, or a team takes a time out.

Each down begins when the ball is snapped, usually to the quarterback.

8

Watchful Officials

Football needs many officials on the field to keep order in the game. Usually called referees, football officials make sure that players don't break the rules. They stop the clock when they see players go out of bounds. They also measure how far a team has moved the ball on each down.

Football officials usually wear back-and-white striped shirts so that they stand out on the field.

Keeping the Game Fair

Officials signal penalties by throwing a colored flag when a rule is broken. The referee usually rewards the other team by moving the ball down the field up to 15 yards. If the offense commits a penalty in their own end zone, the other team is awarded a **safety**, which is worth two points. Penalties can be called on both offensive and defensive players.

Refs use signals to show what is happening. A flag means a penalty. Arms up in the shape of the goal posts means a team has scored.

WARMING UP

Football is a fast and physical game, so it is very important to warm up your body before you play or practice. Football practice usually begins with several warm-up exercises, including jogging, stretching, and **conditioning** exercises, before practicing any plays.

Dynamic Warm-ups

Before any practice or game, all athletes should take at least five to 10 minutes doing general warm-ups. Begin with a light jog to warm up your body. Then do some **dynamic stretching** to prepare your muscles. Static stretches—stretches done while standing still—are better for the end of your workout when your body is loose and warm.

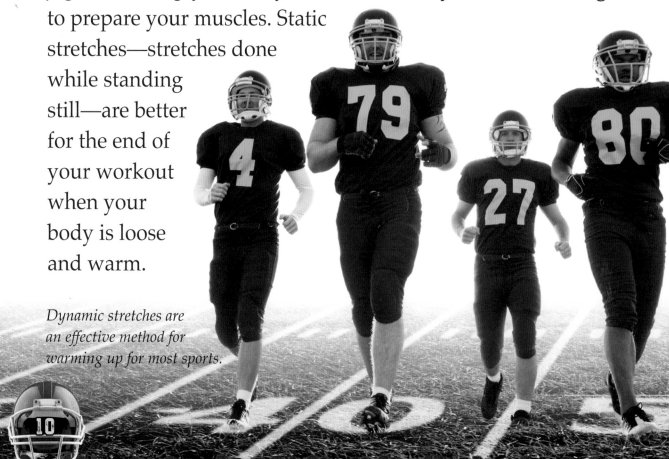

Dynamic stretches are an effective method for warming up for most sports.

Get Moving

Walking lunges, arm swings, hip rotations, and running high knees are among the most common warm-up exercises. Other fun dynamic warm-ups for football include back pedals, inchworms, backward ninjas, and carioca!

◄ *Hip rotations—Lift your knee and rotate your leg out to the side and back to center before stepping forward. Repeat on the other leg as you move forward across the field.*

Arm swings—Stand with your feet ► apart and bend a little at the knees. Keep your arms straight and move them in circles from front to back and back to front. Bend a little at the waist and knees to move with the circles.

Running high knees ► —Run across the field lifting your knees as high as they go. Try to take as many steps as you can. Pump your arms as you lift your knees.

◄*Walking lunges—Step forward with one leg and bend at the knee. Then lift your back leg up to walk forward and bend at the knee again.*

11

RUNNING WITH THE BALL

Football seems like it's all about throwing, catching, and tackling. But the most important skill in football is running. Running backs, quarterbacks, and receivers must all learn how to avoid defensive players while running with the ball. Linebackers and defensive backs must also learn how to block for their teammates on the run or **tackle** their opponents. These players can also pick up a **fumble**, which is a dropped ball, or intercept a pass. Running in football requires sprinting with quick starts and direction changes.

Football players must train their bodies to move with speed and agility.

Securing the Ball

To catch a pass or take a **handoff** you should use both hands and then secure, or hold, the ball against your body. When running you can usually hold it with one hand. Use your hand to hold the ball against your forearm, then tuck your arm to your side to secure the ball against your body.

If you don't hold the ball against your body, defensive players can snatch it away.

Zigzag Drill

Place pylons about 3 to 5 yards (2.7 to 3.7 m) apart in two staggered lines. You will be sprinting around the pylons, moving from one side to the other. At each pylon you will need to turn and change direction or **make a cut**. Keep your body weight centered over your body and use your arms for balance as you cut. As you improve, try to make the cut without taking "stutter steps," or short little steps, to slow down before turning.

Dropping the ball

It's important to keep a good grip on the ball. If a player drops the ball it's called a fumble. Defensive players can cause an offensive player to fumble by knocking the ball from the

Fumbles can change a game quickly. Either side may recover or pick up the ball. Sometimes defenders even score with it!

PASSING THE BALL

Throwing a football can be tricky, especially if your hands are small. Begin with the ball in both hands. The throwing hand should fan out across the ball with the index finger near the tip, your thumb at a right angle to the index finger, and the rest of the fingers over the ball's laces.

Stand with both feet apart and your throwing leg back. Raise the ball up to ear level while holding it in place with the other hand. Pull your throwing shoulder back, then release the throwing arm forward while dropping the other arm and taking a step with the opposite leg. Try to spin the ball on release. This motion is called a **spiral**.

Target Practice

Set up a target that the ball can land inside. Throwing against a wall can damage the ball. Start with something simple, like a large plastic garbage can. You may want to weigh down the garbage can with a sandbag or some rocks. Keep your eyes on the target as you throw. As you improve, move farther and farther away from the target.

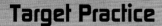

An incomplete pass happens when the quarterback throws the ball but the receiver does not catch it.

Quarterbacks must be able to throw accurately. Regular target practice is the key.

Drew Brees

Quarterback Drew Brees holds six different passing records in the NFL, including the most passes without interceptions in one season. In college, he played for Purdue University in Indiana where he won several awards and still holds many NCAA records. He started his professional career with the San Diego Chargers, and now plays for the New Orleans Saints.

CATCHING THE BALL

Catching a football is a difficult skill to master. It's important to first master catching the ball while standing still before you can learn to catch it while running on the field! Keep your eyes on the tip of the ball by focusing on the crosshairs, where the seams meet. Raise your hands up and form a diamond with your index fingers and thumbs. Catch the ball with your fingers, then squeeze the ball to gain control and hold onto it. When catching a low pass, turn your hands around and touch your pinky fingers together to receive the ball.

Randy Moss

Randy Moss holds the record for the most **touchdown receptions** in a single season with 23 in 2007. He is also the second-best receiver in NFL history with a total of 156 touchdown receptions. Moss played in the NFL for 14 years with several teams, including the Minnesota Vikings and the New England Patriots.

Randy Moss, like many football stars, often helps children and families in need. He has donated food, clothing, and backpacks to schoolchildren.

Catching Drill

Ask your friend or teammate to throw the ball above your head, then to the right of you, and then to the left. Catch the ball with your arms outstretched away from your body with your hands in a diamond formation. Repeat the sequence until you can catch all three consistently. When you're ready, try to catch the ball while running across the field.

Catch and tuck

Because players must tuck the ball into their body before they can run, it may seem like they are catching the ball against their body. But it's important to catch the ball with your hands first, then hold it against your body. Sometimes players try to catch the ball against their chest, forming a bucket with their arms. But a bucket catch is very difficult to control in a game setting—coaches and players don't like it!

Always reach your hands out to catch the ball — don't try to catch it against your body.

17

BLOCKING AND TACKLING

When players use their body to stop another player, it's called blocking. In football, the goal of most players is to block the other team. Offensive linemen or running backs block defensive players to protect the quarterback or the ball carrier. The players on defense use blocks to stop the offense from running their plays. Blocking a player means pushing them or stopping them with your body. You may not grab a player or hold on to any part of them when blocking. A tackle is when a defensive player stops the player with the ball, usually by knocking them down. In a tackle, you can wrap your arms around the player. Normally, this kind of contact is not allowed in elementary-school levels.

Top defenders can make as many as two dozen tackles in a single game.

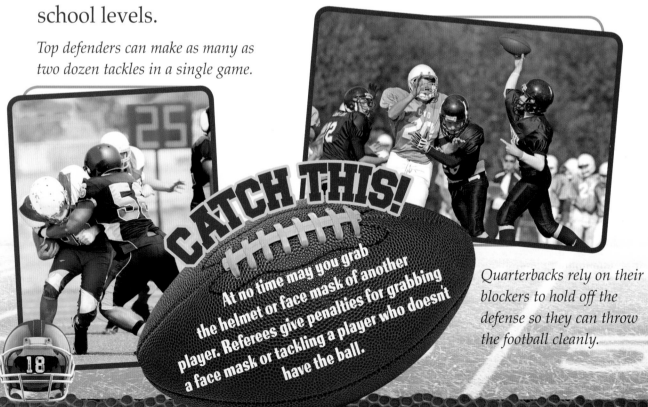

CATCH THIS!

At no time may you grab the helmet or face mask of another player. Referees give penalties for grabbing a face mask or tackling a player who doesn't have the ball.

Quarterbacks rely on their blockers to hold off the defense so they can throw the football cleanly.

Heads Up Tackle

In both blocking and tackling, bending your back and lowering your head increases your risk of injury. Coaches today teach the "heads up tackle" method to help prevent injury. You may only tackle a player in possession of the ball.

The role of defensive players is keeping the offensive players from gaining yards. They do it either by hitting the player hard or by wrapping the player up to limit their movement.

Keep your back straight, your shoulders back, and your head up. Then bend your knees and lean forward slightly. With your body low, take a step in towards the ball carrier, leading with your shoulder. Wrap your arms around the player and drive forward with your legs. As part of the safe tackling process, make sure to never tackle your opponent using your head. Lead the tackle with your shoulder and chest, not with your helmet.

Blocking Drill

To practice blocking with a friend, make a line of scrimmage with a piece of rope or string. Line up opposite your friend at the line of scrimmage. Take turns trying to hold your position as the other tries to push you off balance. Follow your coach's safety instructions for blocking.

19

MIGHTY QUARTERBACKS

The quarterback on a football team is the player in charge of the offense. Quarterbacks start each offensive play by throwing or passing the ball. They have to be great athletes and understand the game very well.

General on the Field

It is also crucial for quarterbacks to show leadership. The coach or offensive coordinator usually calls the plays that a team will run on offense, but the quarterback is responsible for **executing** them. Also, the quarterback must be able to guess how the opposing team's defense will act before a play begins. If quarterbacks see that a play won't work, they must change it on the field. Teams rely on the quarterback to execute plays as skillfully as possible.

Quarterbacks must have a strong, accurate arm for downfield passes.

Playing the Game

The quarterback starts the play after taking the snap from the center. In a running play, the quarterback will hand or **pitch** the ball backward to a running back. In a passing play, the quarterback will try to throw the ball downfield to a wide receiver, tight end, or running back. The quarterback can also run with the ball. The quarterback's role can vary depending on the team's offensive scheme. There are teams that rely on a running game. The quarterback will not throw passes very often. Some teams will rely more on passing. Other teams play both styles.

Not all quarterbacks are tall, but height gives the advantage of seeing the field.

Throwing on the run may be one of the toughest things to do as a quarterback.

Quarterbacks line up directly behind the offensive line at the start of a play.

CATCH THIS!

Peyton Manning of the Denver Broncos set a new record by throwing for 55 touchdowns in one season.

DYNAMIC RECEIVERS

The job of receivers is to catch **forward passes** from the quarterback after the snap. They run down the field to receive passes. They are usually the fastest players on the field and must avoid blocks from defending players. **Tight ends** are receivers who also act as offensive linemen. They are big enough to be blockers on the line of scrimmage, but also fast enough to run down the field and receive forward passes.

Ready to Run

Players are only allowed to receive forward passes if they begin the play on the end of the line of scrimmage or in the **backfield**. **Wide receivers** often start the play behind the line of scrimmage and tight ends start on the outside of the line of scrimmage. Some offensive play **formations** may not include tight ends. If the wide receiver begins on the line of scrimmage, then the tight end acts as a lineman and not a receiver.

Wide receivers usually start from the two-point stance (shown at left), leaning slightly forward with feet apart. Sometimes they use a three-point stance with one hand on the ground.

22

Knowing the Routes

Receivers must learn to run passing patterns. Passing patterns are also called routes and include the slant, the post, the curl, and the swing. But it's also important that the receiver gets open, which means to be in a position that is free of a defensive player. In most passing plays, each receiver runs a different route so the quarterback has some options of who he can pass the ball to.

Defensive players try to anticipate which patterns the offense will be running so that they can prevent receivers from making a catch.

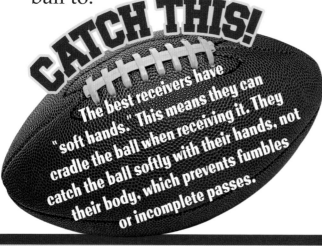

CATCH THIS!

The best receivers have "soft hands." This means they can cradle the ball when receiving it. They catch the ball softly with their hands, not their body, which prevents fumbles or incomplete passes.

Calvin Johnson

Calvin Johnson set the NFL single-season record for most receiving yards in 2012 with 1,964 yards. That's 123 yards per game, more than the length of the field. Johnson has played for the Detroit Lions since he was drafted in 2007. He is big, fast, strong, and agile, and he can jump high to receive passes. This has earned him the nickname Megatron.

Teams count on tall receivers like Calvin Johnson to grab the ball above a crowd of defenders. Johnson stands 6'5" (1.96 m).

EXPLOSIVE RUNNING BACKS

Running backs are members of the offense who start the play in the backfield, with the quarterback. Running backs receive handoffs from the quarterback and then run down the field. This is called **rushing**. Running backs also block defensive players to protect the quarterback or another running back.

Different Roles

A running back's position depends on the team's strategy and the play formation. Fullbacks are usually blockers rather than ball carriers—they play at the very back of the formation. The halfback is the primary ball carrier and traditionally plays halfway between the line of scrimmage and the fullback. When the halfback begins behind the fullback in the formation, the position is often called the tailback.

Emmitt Smith

Emmitt Smith is one of the best running backs in NFL history. He holds the NFL records for the most rushing yards (18,355) and the most rushing touchdowns (164) in a career. Some recruiters thought he was too small to play college football, but he proved them wrong. He went on to win three **Super Bowls** with the Dallas Cowboys and was named Super Bowl MVP in 1994.

Getting the Ball

To receive a handoff from the quarterback, running backs create a pocket with their hands. The quarterback places the ball tight against the running back's belly. Then, one hand and forearm should grasp the ball on top while the other hand and forearm cradles the ball from underneath.

Sometimes running backs may throw a forward pass after receiving a pitch or toss from the quarterback.

Pushing Through

Running backs must be fast and agile to rush the ball down the field and avoid defensive blocks. They usually hold the ball in one arm and use the other arm to push defensive players out of the way as they run. Running backs must also provide offensive blocks to defend the quarterback and the other running backs. Teams with strong running backs play a running game. After the quarterback, the halfback or tailback is often the biggest star on the field.

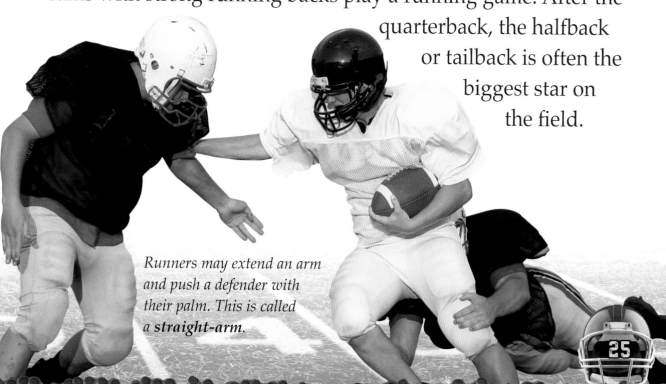

*Runners may extend an arm and push a defender with their palm. This is called a **straight-arm**.*

25

POWERFUL LINEMEN

Offensive linemen protect the quarterback on passing plays and create holes in the defensive line for running plays. They push the defensive lineman either back or to the side. There are five linemen that must line up the same way for every play: a center, two guards on either side, and two offensive tackles next to the guards. The players in these positions are not allowed to catch forward passes and they cannot move more than two yards beyond the line of scrimmage.

Linemen play on the line of scrimmage. They are usually the largest players on the field and must be very good at blocking opposing players.

CATCH THIS!

When a defensive lineman tackles a quarterback before he can throw a pass, it is called a sack. Defensive players are always putting pressure on quarterbacks to force them to pass before they're ready.

Stopping the Ball

Defensive linemen play opposite the offensive linemen. Their job is to block the offensive linemen so their teammates can stop the quarterback or the running backs. Defensive linemen may also tackle the ball carrier. The defensive line is made up of defensive tackles and defensive ends. Defensive linemen are usually a little smaller and faster than offensive linemen, because they need to do more running during the play.

The Center

The center lineman takes the ball to the line of scrimmage. The quarterback starts behind the center. After they call the plays, quarterbacks call "hike" and centers snap the ball between their legs to the quarterbacks. Snapping the ball is a special skill—if quarterbacks miss the ball or lose their grip, the team may lose yards.

27

RUTHLESS LINEBACKERS

Linebacker is a defensive position that begins a few yards behind the line of scrimmage. This player's job is to tackle the person running with the ball. Linebackers must be strong and fast. They must be ready to defend against both passing and running plays. They also put pressure on the opposing quarterback to prevent successful passes.

Linebackers cover the field and make many key defensive plays. They usually lead their teams in the number of tackles made in each game.

Middle linebackers

Middle linebackers play in the middle of the line of scrimmage and outside linebackers play the outside of the line. The middle linebacker is often called the "quarterback of defense," because they call the defensive plays. Outside linebackers are sometimes called right and left outside linebackers or strong side and weak side linebackers.

When a linebacker runs through the line of scrimmage to sack the quarterback, it's called a blitz.

28

Defensive backs

Defensive backs play farther back from the line of scrimmage. They defend against the wide receivers and tight ends to stop them from catching forward passes. Defensive backs also tackle any ball carriers that get

When trying to break up a pass, linebackers sometimes intercept the ball.

past the linemen and linebackers. Defensive backs may be called safeties, cornerbacks, or in Canadian football, defensive halfbacks. Th number of players in the defensive back position depends on a coach's defensive strategy.

Most linebackers start from a two-point stance which allows them to react quickly.

Luke Kuechly

Luke Kuechly is an NFL linebacker for the Carolina Panthers. He led the NFL in tackles in 2014 and in 2012—his rookie season. In 2013, Kuechly won the Defensive Player of the Year award. He played football at Boston College where he was an All-American.

Luke Kuechly, born in 1991, became the youngest winner of the NFL Defensive Player of the Year in 2013.

SPORTSMANSHIP

Football is a very physical game and players must be aggressive. This can lead to conflict both on and off the field, which makes good sportsmanship very important. After a game, teams and their coaches shake hands. The captains of opposing teams also shake hands before the coin toss, which determines which team gets possession of the ball first.

Good football players must be very team-oriented. While quarterbacks, running backs, and wide receivers are often the stars of the game, they still rely on their teammates. Football teams also need many backup players who may never play in a game, but must always be ready in case a teammate is injured. It is important that teams stay positive and focus on taking pride in hard work and team unity.

Nutrition

Football games and practice sessions are very demanding and players sweat a lot. In fact, many coaches weigh their players before and after practice sessions to track how much water weight they lose, since too much is unhealthy. Players must stay hydrated. It's important to drink water before, during, and after playing. Players should also replace the salt and potassium they lose when they sweat. Athletes need to eat extra **calories** because they use more energy. But, they also need the right calories. It's important to choose foods with lots of nutrients and good quality carbohydrates and proteins.

LEARNING MORE

Check out these books and websites to find out more about the game.

Books

Football: How It Works by Agnieszka Biskup. c. 2010, Capstone Press

The Everything Kids' Football Book by Greg Jacobs. c. 2014, Adams Media

Play Football Like a Pro by Matt Doeden. c. 2010, Capstone Press

Websites

USA Football

www.usafootball.com

The governing body for amateur football in the United States.

Football Canada

www.footballcanada.com/

The governing body for amateur football in Canada.

Pop Warner Football

www.popwarner.com/football

This site has information about joining a team and staying safe as you play.

GLOSSARY

Some **boldfaced** words are defined where they appear in the text.

backfield The area of the field that is behind the line of scrimmage

calories How the amount of energy in food is measured

conditioning exercises Series of workouts an athlete performs to be in proper physical shape for the specific sport

contact sport A sport where players come into contact with each other

downs A chance for the team to advance the ball down the field

dynamic stretching Stretching that happens while moving the body rather than standing or sitting

end zone The scoring area on either side of the football field

execute To perform or carry out

field goal A goal scored by kicking the ball through the goal posts

first down When the team gains 10 yards and gets another four or three downs

formation The way the players set themselves up on the line of scrimmage

forward pass A pass thrown from behind the line of scrimmage towards the opponent's goal

gridiron A metal frame made of parallel bars

handoff When the quarterback gives the ball to a running back

hashmarks Small, regularly spaced markings

incomplete pass When a receiver misses the pass

interception When a defensive player catches the pass

kickoff A play that occurs at the beginning of the game, after halftime, or after a scoring play by the offense to resume play

line of scrimmage When both teams line up along the yard line

pitch A short pass, often back or to the side, or the act of making the pass

rushing Gain of yards by running with the ball

safety A scoring play that results in two points being awarded to the scoring team

single or rouge A single point scored in Canadian football by kicking the ball into the end zone

snap The action that begins each play in a football game, except for the kickoff

special teams The players who handle kickoffs, field goals, and punts

spiral When the football spins tightly as it's thrown

straight-arm An action where a player pushes a potential tackler away by holding the arm out straight

Super Bowl The championship game of the National Football League

tackle When one player stops another, especially by knocking the opponent to the ground

touchdown reception When a player catches or receives the pass and then makes a touchdown

INDEX